CHANGES IN
FOOD AND
FARMING

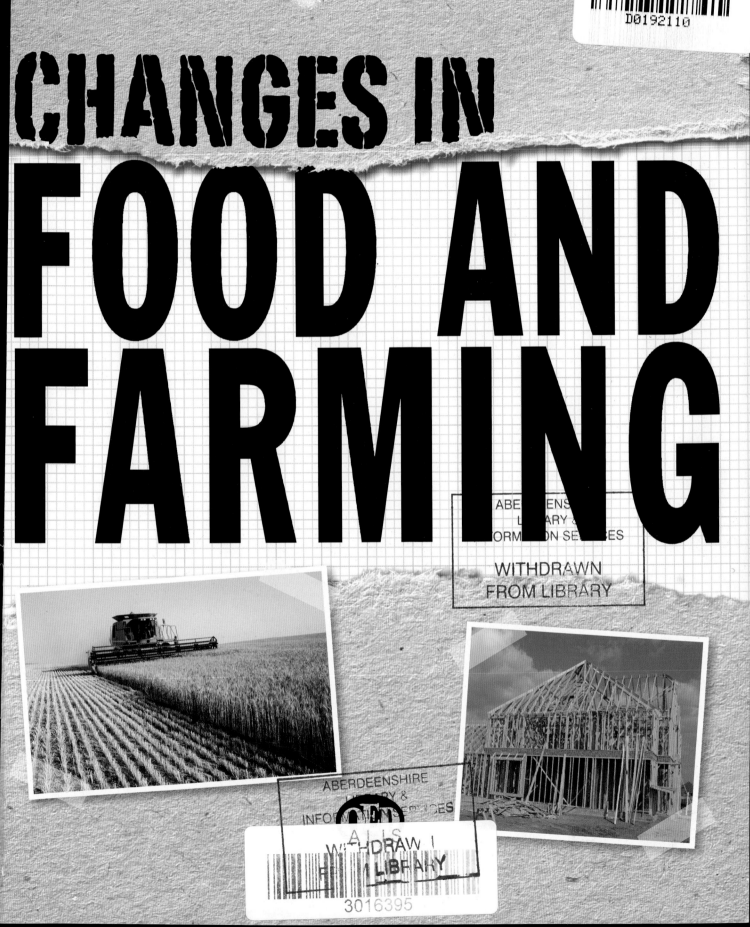

First published in the UK in 2009 by
QED Publishing
A Quarto Group Company
226 City Road
London EC1V 2TT
www.qed-publishing.co.uk

ISBN 978 1 84835 242 1

Author Steve Parker
Consultant Terry Jennings
Project Editor Anya Wilson
Design and Picture Research Dynamo Design

Publisher Steve Evans
Creative Director Zeta Davies
Managing Editor Amanda Askew

Printed and bound in China

The words in **bold**
are explained in the
glossary on page 30.

Contents

DOWN ON the farm

Thousands of years ago, there were no farms. People collected wild fruits and other plants, and hunted wild animals to eat. These hunter-gatherers never settled in one place – they moved around the land to find food.

Without machines, early farmers developed pumping systems for water.

⟳Before animals were **domesticated**, people had to **plough** the land.

A great change

About 15,000 to 12,000 years ago, there was a great change. People began to put wild plant seeds such as wheat, barley, oats and rice in the ground. As the plants grew, the people **harvested**, or gathered, their grains and other products to eat and store. They chose seeds from the best plants to grow the year after, which improved their **crops**.

Domesticating animals

People also began to keep sheep, goats, pigs and cows, for their milk, meat, fur and skins. Gradually the wild animals became domesticated, or tamed, as **livestock**. As this happened, people began to stay in one place. They built villages and looked after their fields and livestock. They were the first farmers.

⋔ *Strong cows called oxen ploughed the fields of early farms.*

It's a wonder!

Huge machines such as **combine harvesters** do the work of 100 people.

Farming gives us much more food than collecting from the wild. The number of people in the world has gone up from five million about 10,000 years ago to almost 7000 million today.

Growing food

Every minute, nearly 250 babies are born around the world, and so there are more people to feed. As the number of people grows, better farms are needed to produce enough food.

Big business

In some regions, such as the United States of America, farms are more like factories. Growing crops and raising livestock are industries with enormous machines such as tractors, harvesters, helicopters and planes. Farm fields stretch further than you can see. These farms produce much more food than those in poorer regions.

Small farms

In some places of the world, such as in parts of Africa, farms are small. If the weather is bad and crops fail, people may struggle to grow enough to feed themselves. If the weather is good, farmers can grow enough to feed their families and perhaps some extra to sell at market.

In some parts of China, rice is harvested by hand.

↻ This area of farmland in California, USA, is 2000 square kilometres in area. It is divided into squares, like many modern farms, to make the land easier to farm.

📷 **FOCUS ON**

Livestock
Many different animals are bred on farms around the world. They are used to work in the fields as well as to supply meat, dairy, wool, fur and leather.

In South America, guinea pigs are bred for their meat.

FERTILE land

In some places, farms are very successful and grow lots of crops. In others, the soil is not fertile or the weather is bad, and less food can be produced.

Good for farms

There are good farming conditions across most of Europe, in parts of Asia, and in much of North America, southern South America, New Zealand and eastern Australia. Crops grow well, and there are fields of **grassland** for livestock.

❂In the United States of America, corn is the most highly produced crop. It is mainly used for food and **biofuel**.

❂Fruit orchards thrive with plenty of rich soil, water and sunshine.

Difficult to grow

Some parts of Africa, Asia and South America are too wet for farming. Much of North Africa, the Middle East and central Australia is too dry. All around the far north of the world is covered in ice and snow. It is difficult for people in these places to grow enough food.

It's a wonder!

Good soil is very important for farmers. They need to **preserve** it or crops will fail.

About four-fifths of the world's land is unsuitable for farming. Everyone relies on the remaining one-fifth, so farmers take good care of it.

Farming wood

Farms do not just produce food. They provide many other things that people use every day, such as tea and coffee. Trees are also harvested on farms to produce wood.

So many uses

Wood from trees is used in endless ways, from building houses, sheds and bridges to making beds, tables, chairs and artwork. Trees are also **pulped**, crushed and mixed with water, to make materials such as paper, which we use in books and newspapers.

↻ It can take more than 100 trees to build one timber-frame house.

↻ Pulped trees are used in this factory to produce rolls of paper.

Wood farms

In many places, trees are planted as crops. These places, called timber **plantations**, are wood farms. After many years, the trees are cut down for their wood. Then more trees are planted to replace them. Using wood in this way is **sustainable** – we can grow new supplies so they do not run out. The problem is that some trees are cut down in wild forests and not replaced, and so there are now fewer trees in the world.

It's a wonder!

In the United States, four million trees are planted every day to replace those cut down.

NATURE in danger

Some trees are difficult to farm on plantations as they take hundreds of years to grow. Instead they are cut down from wild places such as tropical rainforests. This damages the homes of wildlife.

Tropical trees

Some of the strongest, most beautiful wood comes from tropical forests, where it is warm all year round. They are known as tropical hardwoods and include teak, mahogany, ebony and rosewood. Products made from these woods are sold for lots of money.

⊂ One tropical tree, such as the redwood, can be home to thousands of types of wildlife.

Hotspots

Tropical forests are also 'hotspots' for wildlife, with very high biodiversity – the variety of animals and plants. As the trees are cut down, animals have nowhere to live and the wildlife disappears. This can lead to extinction, as wildlife has nowhere to live and breed.

More than 200 types of monkey, such as this squirrel monkey, are threatened by forest devastation.

⮑ Timber from trees is loaded onto trucks and taken to sawmills.

Double disaster

As tropical forests are cut down for their valuable wood, many other changes happen. The whole natural area, or habitat, may be destroyed.

⟳This hillside in the Andes, Ecuador, was once covered in trees. The soil is slowly being washed away.

Washed away

As trees grow upwards, their roots grow down into the soil. The roots help to hold the soil and stop it washing away in the rain. If the trees and their roots are taken away, especially in a rainforest, the heavy rain carries the soil away into the rivers. The land is left bare and no more plants can grow.

⟳Floods caused by overflowing rivers ruin farm crops and destroy buildings.

FOCUS ON

Disappearing forests

Tropical forests once covered one-seventh of the world's land. Now they only cover one-seventeenth. Unless we slow the damage, most of them could be gone in 40 years, along with the animals and plants that live there.

Forest is cleared in Brazil for farmers to grow soya crops to sell.

Damaging floods

As the soil washes away, it clogs rivers. The water cannot flow properly and floods the riverbanks, causing damage to surrounding farms and living space.

When soil washes into rivers, fish suffer because they cannot breathe properly or find enough food.

Make way for farms

As more farms are needed in the world to produce enough food for people, they take over wild places, and local plants and animals have nowhere to live.

Forest to farm

New farms are often built in cleared forest areas. If the soil washes away, the crops sometimes fail. People then move and clear more wild areas to set up new farms. This causes the damage to quickly spread.

Rice fields, or paddies, need lots of water, taken from nearby lakes.

Wet to dry

Other habitats that are in danger of disappearing are swamps, marshes and other wetlands. Ditches and canals are dug to take away the water to make the soil drier and more suitable for farming. Wetland plants and animals such as frogs, fish, alligators and cranes lose their homes. More than half the world's wetlands have been lost in the past 100 years.

Frogs, such as the African bullfrog, may become endangered in the future if their wetland habitat dries out.

☟ Large birds, such as pelicans, suffer if their water habitats are cleared for farming because they have nowhere to live.

It's a wonder!

On **migration**, many birds must stop over at wetlands.

In 2006, 120 countries in North America, Europe, Africa and West Asia started Wings Over Wetlands, or WOW. They aim to save wetlands where migrating birds stop to rest and feed.

ENDLESS fields

Some farm fields stretch as far as you can see. They grow plenty of food. However, wildlife can suffer as land is taken over for farms.

Is big better?

Large fields mean more crops can be grown. Modern farms have tractors to plough the soil, seed drills for planting and harvesters to gather crops. These machines are large and need space, so farmers cut down hedges and trees that get in their way. Fewer trees and hedges mean animals have nowhere to shelter.

Combine harvesters can clear a huge field in a few hours.

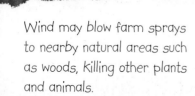

Wind may blow farm sprays to nearby natural areas such as woods, killing other plants and animals.

Chemical sprays

Some farmers spray their crops to protect them from pests that eat the crops. The **chemical** sprays not only kill pests, but they can also harm animals such as butterflies and birds. The chemicals spread to the soil and water, causing **pollution**.

Good farming

Farmers can change the crop in a field every year. This is called crop rotation. It keeps the soil healthy and reduces pests. Planting hedges gives shelter to birds and other creatures that eat the pests on crops.

Fields are ploughed to turn over the top layer of the soil, bringing fresh nutrients to the surface.

⊃ By growing different crops, different nutrients are added to the soil.

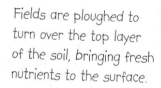

⊃ Organic food may taste better than food grown with chemicals and sprays.

ALL ORGANIC PRODUCE

'Organic' vegetables and fruits are grown in ways that are good for wildlife and the soil. Have a look in your local store or supermarket for organic labels.

Wht Cn U do ?

Hi-tech farming

On farms, cows, pigs and chickens used to wander freely in the fields. Now, farmers need to change the way animals are kept because we need more food and therefore more space, which we don't have.

Indoor animals

On many modern farms, animals are kept indoors. A smaller space is used compared to an outside area, and more food, such as meat and eggs, can be produced. Cows and pigs live in big barns and chickens stay in sheds. They are kept warm and fed specially made food.

New crops

Scientists can alter farm crops by changing the genes – tiny chemical 'instructions' inside them that control how they grow. This is called **genetic modification**, or GM. GM crops may be able to grow in poor soil and not be destroyed by pests, so more food is produced.

Genetically modified cotton can also be grown. This gives farmers a better crop to sell.

'Free-range' farm animals can wander in yards or fields, rather than being kept indoors. Look for 'free-range' labels on eggs, chicken, pork and other meat products.

⊂Instead of being kept in fields, cows sometimes live in barns.

Free-range chickens roam freely outside.

Farming the sea

Farms are not just on land. They are in water, too. Many kinds of fish are farmed for us to eat. They can be taken from the sea or special fish farms.

○In some areas, overfishing has meant there are hardly any fish for boats to catch.

Fishing fleets

Many kinds of wild fish are caught in the oceans, such as sardines, tuna, cod and salmon, and shellfish such as mussels, crabs and prawns. Modern fishing boats are so big and effective that in some areas they have caught too many fish. There are none left to breed. This is known as **overfishing**. It will take many years for fish numbers to become high again.

Captive fish

Wild fish can also be farmed in huge tanks on land, and in giant cages floating in the sea. The fish are well fed, grow fast and are easy to catch. Sometimes they may suffer diseases from being too crowded.

➲ *Salmon are raised in massive cages in lakes and along coasts.*

📷 FOCUS ON

Bycatch

Dolphins, seals and other animals are sometimes caught accidentally as 'bycatch' in fishing nets. This has helped to cause some species, such as sea turtles, to become endangered.

Some species of sea turtles are endangered because large numbers of them die when they get caught in nets.

Energy farms

Some farm crops are grown as a source of energy. They are burned for heating and cooking, as fuels in vehicles, and in power stations to make electricity. They are known as biofuels.

↻Corn is one of the most widely grown crops in the world. A lot of it is grown in the USA and China.

Biofuels

Some biofuels come from plants with oily seeds, such as palm, sunflower, soya and canola (rapeseed). The seeds are squeezed or pressed to remove the oil, which is treated with chemicals and burned, for example, as biodiesel. Other biofuels such as sugar cane are left to ferment, or rot. They produce gases such as methane or liquids such as ethanol, which are burned to produce energy.

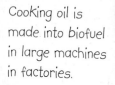
Cooking oil is made into biofuel in large machines in factories.

Sustainable fuels

We use a lot of **fossil fuels** – coal, oil and gas – and they are running out. Biofuels are sustainable – we can replace them by growing new crops every year. Biofuel plants such as sugar cane also take in the **greenhouse gas** carbon dioxide as they grow, which helps to reduce **global warming**.

A vehicle needs to be changed to work with biofuel, which can be bought at some filling stations.

These soya bean fields in Brazil were once tropical rainforest.

📷 FOCUS ON

Biofuel problems

Biofuel crops may be grown on land that was once a natural habitat, meaning wildlife has been destroyed or lost its home. Or they can be grown on land once used for food crops, so local people cannot farm.

Mountains and miles

Some places have successful farms and grow too much food. Other places don't have enough food. This is because of different farming conditions.

Too much food

Successful farmers have 'food mountains' of produce such as wheat and potatoes. The farmer has to pay huge costs to store these foods properly, keep them free of pests and disease, and transport them to faraway places where people lack food. Sometimes the spare food ends up being ploughed back into the soil.

Giant grain tanks are used to store crops until they are sold.

➔ If food is not sold, sometimes it is left to rot.

World travel

In a big food store, you can buy all kinds of fruit, vegetable, spices, meat and other food from around the world. Transporting these by ship, plane, train and truck uses up fuel energy and other resources. It adds to problems of pollution and global warming. Foods grown locally mean fewer 'food miles' and fewer problems for the natural world.

Moving animals over long distances costs money. This adds to the price of meat.

Wht Cn U do?

Look at fruit, vegetable and meat labels in a supermarket to see where they come from. Visit a local farmers' market, where the foods are usually grown nearby and stored for less time. It is better to choose foods that do not travel far.

Local market produce is often sold shortly after it has been harvested.

Keeping shelves full

Millions of people around the world are starving, and suffering from diseases caused by lack of food and clean water. As the number of people increases, these problems may get worse.

Enough for everyone

The world's farmers can produce enough food to feed everyone, but this food isn't shared equally around the world. The main problem is that many people do not have enough land to grow food, or enough money to buy it.

⏷ Stocks of food aid are piled up to be sent to the village of Yama in northwestern Niger.

Climate and farming

Global warming is caused mainly by carbon dioxide gas, which is produced by burning fossil fuels. It will alter the weather and cause climate change. This could cause farming areas to suffer floods, droughts, storms and other problems. Also some kinds of farming use lots of machinery, energy, materials and other resources, which is not sustainable. More natural ways of farming help to reduce these problems.

When farmland is flooded, crops are usually ruined. This costs the farmer money.

It's a wonder!

In 1992, the number of very hungry people in the world was about 850 million. In 2002, it had gone down to 820 million.

Refugees line up in Darfur, Africa, to receive food aid donated by other countries.

Glossary

Biodiversity The range or variety of different living things found in one habitat or place.

Biofuel A fuel made from a plant. It supplies energy, usually by burning, which gives off heat.

Bycatch When fish or other water animals are caught accidentally, usually by being trapped in nets, and are not the creatures intended to be caught.

Chemical In crop sprays, a substance that is used to kill certain living things, such as weeds, moulds or insect pests.

Combine harvester A farming machine that combines several harvesting jobs, such as cutting a crop and separating the wanted parts – seeds – from the unwanted parts – stems.

Crops Plants grown and harvested (gathered) by people for many purposes, such as rice, wheat and potatoes for food, or straw for making thatched roofs, or sugar cane to make biofuel.

Domesticated Plants and animals that are mostly tame. They are used to farm crops and as pets.

Extinction When a type of animal or plant has died out completely so that there is none left anywhere in the world.

Fertile In farming, soil that has plenty of nutrients and goodness, so that crops grow well in it.

Fossil fuel The remains of a once-living thing, which died long ago. It was buried and preserved in the rocks.

Genetic modification, GM Altering the natural genes or chemical 'instructions' inside a living thing, such as adding a gene to make it grow faster.

Global warming The rise in the Earth's temperature due to increased amounts of greenhouse gases in the atmosphere.

Grassland A place such as the North American prairies or African savanna, where the main plants are grasses, rather than trees, bushes, cactus or other plants.

Greenhouse gas A gas that helps to take in the Sun's heat and make the atmosphere around Earth warmer.

Habitat A particular kind of place or surrounding where animals and plants live, such as a lake, river, wood, desert, seashore or coral reef.

Harvest To gather or collect plant parts such as fruits, especially for food, and also for other uses, such as harvesting reeds to make thatch for roofs.

Hotspot A popular place.

Livestock Farm animals that are domesticated (tamed) and are kept for their meat, fur or hair, skins, milk and pulling power.

Migration When birds or other animals travel regularly from one part of the world to another.

Organic In farming, crops and livestock that are raised in a mainly natural way, without artificial chemicals such as pesticides and fertilizers.

Overfishing Catching too many fish or other water animals from an area, so there are not enough left to breed and carry on their kind.

Plantations Areas planted by people with the same kind of crop, usually a type of tree, such as oil palm trees for palm oil, or spruce trees for timber (wood).

Plough To turn over the soil by pulling along a large curved metal blade before planting seeds.

Pollution When harmful substances such as chemicals or litter get into the surroundings and cause damage.

Preserve To save something from being destroyed or harmed.

Pulp To crush something until it almost becomes a liquid.

Sustainable Something that can carry on for a very long time, without running out or wearing away.

Tropical rainforest A large area of trees, situated in areas around the middle of Earth on either side of the Equator. It rains on most days throughout the year.

Index